ISBN: 979-8-9883780-0-6

Written and Designed by Christine Billingsley and Stephanie Travis

For more information on Cyber Snackz™, visit cybersnackz.org

Meet the TOY BOX

World Class Cyber Team

>Inbox: New Message

>

>Hi,

>Welcome to the Toy Box!

We are a group of pets that like to play with computers.

Come join us on our adventures as we learn about the cyber world.

Peace, Love, and Hacking,

– the Toy Box

>

>END TRANSMISSION

Cyber Snackz ™

Cookies

Fangz

HOpps

Cra$h

Flash Drive

RazOr

CYBER SNACKZ™

Leader of the Toy Box

Classification: Dog
Breed: Pomeranian
Interests: Snacking and Hacking
Dinosaurs
Fishing and Outdoors

FLASH DRIVE

Flashy Troublemaker

Classification: Dog
Breed: Pug
Interests: Flashy Things
DJing
Napping

FANGZ

Fast and Curious Feline

Classification: Cat
Breed: Turkish Angora
Interests: Social Engineering
Video Games & Card Games
Flying Drones

COOKIES
A Little Sweet, a Lot of Smart

Classification: Dog
Breed: Dachshund
Interests: Baking
Outer Space
Tinkering

Classification: Dog
Breed: Labrador
Interests: Learning
Reading
Diving

RAZOR
On the Cutting Edge

INTERNET

The Internet is a large network that connects computers all over the world. Through the Internet people can share information and communicate from anywhere with an internet connection.

People connect to the Internet in many ways.

INTERNET OF THINGS

The Internet of things is a term for electronic devices connected to the Internet but aren't traditional computers.

HACKERS

Hackers are people who use their computer skills to overcome challenges. Some hackers try to get into computers that they are not supposed to get into while other hackers work to make computers more secure against other hackers.

THINK LIKE AN ADVERSARY

What types of thoughts would a possible attacker have? In the bubbles, fill in what they might be thinking about. Remember, attackers want to see things you don't want them to see.

DEFENSE IN DEPTH

A strategy of including multiple layers of security within a system so that if one layer fails, another layer of security is already in place to stop the attack or unauthorized access.

Label the different layers of protection that Fange has on the playground.

PHISHING

Phishing is when attackers send sneaky emails that are designed to trick people into providing data or downloading bad software.

From: support@paw-talk.co
To: CyberSnackz@toybox.com

This is a confirmation that the password for your PawTok account CyberSnackz has just been changed.

If this is your PawTok account but you didn't request a password change, you can reset your password here.

If you're having trouble, please refer to the PawTok Help Center.

MALWARE

Malware is a program or file that is intentionally harmful to a computer.

Malware is delivered to unsuspecting users in many ways. One of the attackers' main tactics is to attach their malware to phishing emails.

MALWARE MAZE

> Inbox: New Mission

>

> Classification: Top Secret

> Help Snackz get through the circuit maze to install antivirus software.

> Be sure to avoid the Malware!

>

> END TRANSMISSION

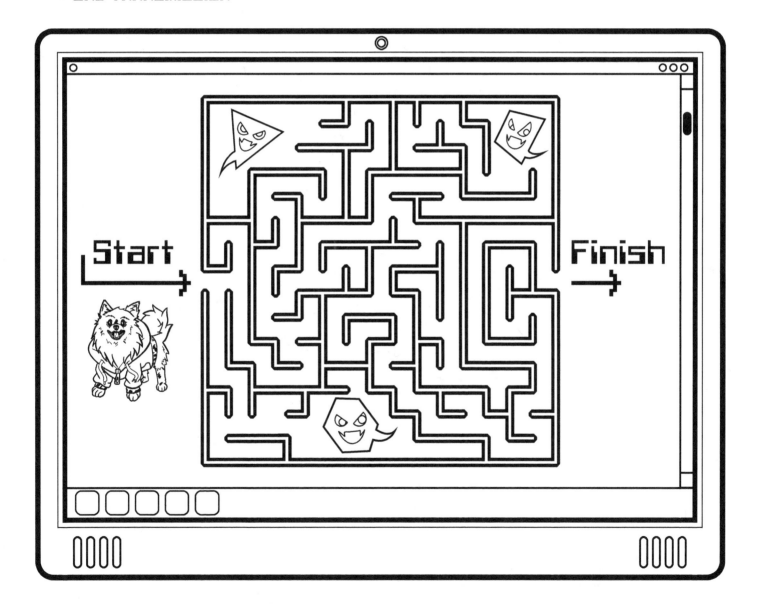

RANSOMWARE

Ransomware is a special kind of malware that prevents users from accessing the files on their devices unless they pay the hackers money.

BINARY ACTIVITY

Binary is a way of counting where each place in the number is 0 or 1. This is the way that computers communicate with each other at the lowest level! To convert the binary number to base 10, the way we normally count, you add up the places that have a one! Check out the table below – everywhere that has a 1 is part of the number we're representing!

128	64	32	16	8	4	2	1
0	0	1	1	0	1	1	0

32 + 16 + 4 + 2 = 54! So... 00110110 in binary is 54 in base 10!

Now it's your turn – fill in the grid below to reveal a cool picture! The numbers across the top of the grid are the same as the numbers at the top of the table above. The numbers down the side tell you what number you're trying to represent in binary!

	128	64	32	16	8	4	2	1
54			■	■		■	■	
247								
193								
28								
60								
126								
255								
111								

THINK BEFORE YOU CLICK

Before you click on messages, make sure you know who they are being sent from.

Did you expect them to send the link or attachment? Does the link or attachment look like something they would send you?

Links or attachments you were not expecting could be a way for an adversary to send you malware.

Hey! We saw you liked a video about The Toy Box! You'll love this new app!

Send us a picture of the download and we'll pay you $10. Respond with a pic of the download.

Great! We will send you a $10 gift card. What's your email address?

STRONG PASSWORDS

Strong passwords are important to keep accounts safe.

- ☐ At least 12 characters long
- ☐ Avoid common words
- ☐ Use uppercase and lowercase characters, numbers, and symbols
- ☐ Not commonly used like "password" or "123456"
- ☐ Use a phrase to help remember your password.
        Ex. Twinkle"Twinkle"LittleStar!"

Please create an example of a strong password using these guidelines.

Enter your password:

CONFIDENTIALITY

Private information is not disclosed unless authorized to access the information.

Make an " x " on the statements that RazOr should keep confidential.

SOCIAL MEDIA

Most peole spend a lot of time on the Internet using social media.

Social media are applications that allow you to share thoughts, pictures, and videos with your friends and followers.

It is important to remember all of the things we've talked about so that you can have fun and use the internet safely, and with permission of your parents or guardian.

INTERNET SAFETY PLEDGE

Say the pledge with Cyber Snackz™ to promise to be safe online.

Then sign on the line below.

☐ I will think before I click

☐ I will not share personal information

☐ When in doubt, I will ask a trusted adult

✕ _____

[Sign Here]